Hansha
Words can Heal or Break

Alta H Haffner 2024
ALL RIGHTS RESERVED

ISBN: 978-0-7961-6770-5

Our words can heal or break! Take care of the words you speak. Take care of the hurt you feel.

M H Haffner

"In the pursuit of healing and accepting"

About the Author

Alta H Haffner is an author, poet, editor, and publisher. Her passion for the written word led her to start three international poetry magazines, Poets Unlimited, Haiku for Your Soul, and Accepting Grief, and is now combined into one magazine called "The Sakura Magazine" What began as a stress-relieving hobby has now blossomed into a full-time career, living a life blessed with a poetic voice.

Alta takes great pleasure in helping new writers achieve their publishing dreams by designing aesthetically pleasing books and getting them published on various platforms, such as Amazon. She also hosts two podcasts, one where she interviews authors from around the world, and the other where she showcases her own poetry collections.

From savoring a quiet morning coffee to admiring the beauty of moonlit skies, Alta remains committed to pursuing her dreams. She draws her invigorating inspiration from the South African sunrise, where she lives with her loving husband, poet/writer Charles R Haffner and continues to explore the depth of thought through her writing. In all her endeavors, she remains dedicated to her dream and shows up for it every day.

Poetic Blessings

About the Book

"In the
pursuit of healing
and accepting".

We have all been sad, angry and hurt and it is a constant journey to accepting all our great life lessons.

In this book I explore emotions and reflections based on the poetic form "Hansha" created by Alta H Haffner

alta@sakurabookpublishing.com

tears fall at first dawn
a night of terror
dreams are not always pleasant

communication
days of blurred memories
motherhood hurts now

silenced by my blood
I have my thoughts now
rusted tears at the ocean

tears hold my secrets
calm my anxious mind
the world slowly fades away

cold whispered secrets
moment of calmness
tranquil tears in a cold breeze

the burdens of life
leaves me all alone
embraced in sweet solitude

words can heal or break

soul bleeds on paper

poetic intimacy

counting syllables
the deepest journey
finding solace through my words

connecting bridges
accepting my fate
walls separating us now

bearing all broken
write three lines of hope
even if no forgiveness

vivid memories
I slowly accept
one day he will need me more

sleepless nights I pray
for happier thoughts
I confess to the heavens

sorrowful tears fall
once beautiful bond
darkest cloud over my soul

withered pink blossoms
melancholy songs
my heart breaking at sunset

navigating hurt

sunset misery

emotionally pensive

a new chapter starts
accepting their wish
space and time may not heal me

sadness will break you
look deeply within
your frown won't last forever

sky full of darkness
sorrowful tears fall
scream to the heavens above

in my aging grace
fearful morning thoughts
nothing matters anymore

exhausted panic
crushing hopelessness
another day of this war

they are happier
trying not to care
needed more words to explain

motherhood betrayal
I gave my soft soul
left with a broken heart now

*I have given all
hurtful words echo
while they sleep so peacefully*

assumption kills peace
hurtful stab of words
decades of healing words fade

a puddle of tears
words drowning my soul
another dark sleepless night

harsh words unspoken
stabbing me soul deep
souvenirs of my old self

a soft broken soul
words are evidence
a heart full of hopefulness

dark heavy rainstorms
matching my chaos
while the smell calms me soul deep

a thunderous storm
dust soaking up tears
absorbing no happiness

the world within me
fights with the outside
always rest in peacefulness

looking at the snow
tears cold as winter
jasmine tea soothing my soul

a thunderous storm
breathe in and exhale
embrace the night sky with love

forget all the pain
look to Sakura
a garden of hope blooming

inner core soulful
exhale and forgive
peace and harmony within

shed the bitterness
cry and let it be
blow it into winters breeze

early windy dusk
moon above willow
rainbow of sorrows linger

brittle winter leaves
sunshine greets my tears
a handful of hope remains

forgive completely
pain gives you lessons
a reason to understand

anger needs no words
show them empathy
hate is toxic to your soul

heal through memories
it will be painful
talk about it scream loudly

finally at peace
decades of sorrow
a fullmoon greets shiny stars

pumpkin spice ice cream
indulging flavor
the little things that matters

midnight rendezvous
lips kissing till dawn
dancing in the summer rain

stargazing lovers
entangled love words
the ocean breeze through our hair

true love always wins
you fill my dark pages
with pure love and acceptance

cuddles in winter

our forevermore

endless summer ocean walks

hold my hand softly
lets sit in silence
just pondering on our hearts

*unconditionally
you loved my soul first
with every unspoken word*

*I stare at the moon
no turning back now
as you softly kiss my smile*

matcha moonlight drink
love forevermore
as the stas glistens brightly

moonlight greeting love
awakening hearts
surrounded by the bright stars

petals blossoming
the break of sunrise
romantic Sakura path

as the fireflies dance
dark storm clouds floating
an old well granting wishes

bright amber sunrise
sipping black coffee
butterflies feast on petals

summer rainfall dawn
traces across my heart
glowing colorful rainbow

skies of dusty dusk
stars greeting lovers
halfmoon hiding between clouds

ancient syllables
our tranquility
the language of peace

scarlet petals fall
nature's earth nourished
muddy ground covered with gifts

enchanted temple
sitting Buddha greets
cold frosted emerald path

glistening sunrise
melted memories
white mountain snow horizon

moonlit covered path
gifts to behold now
distant temple bell echoes

beautiful autumn
soak up life's moments
rusty leaves falling slowly

meadows of blossoms
Hanami at dawn
the beauty of tiny buds

boats rowing slowly
crickets sing 'til dawn
fishing under the moonlight

lanterns burning bright

Sakura backdrop

breathtaking Hirosaki

tranquil and peaceful

heaven reflected

a river of memories

the starry sky greets
i'm dancing in hope
while watching amber sunsets

a thick blanket folds
covered icy snow
soft pastel pink Sakura

evergreen grasslands
leaves falling so slow
happy birds sing their duets

pretty butterfly
waiting for the sun
contemplating for rainfall

a plum blossom greets
while birds sit and wait
infinite beauty at dawn

sowing my sorrows
gentle waves of hope
lonely boat returns to shore

self discovery
my renewed journey
even during a dark night

snow falling slowly
a peaceful silence
crackling fire keeping me warm

time to take it slow
hear my soothing words
hold on to precious moments

through all my dark storms
silence is better
letting go is easier

river flowing down
moment to reflect
dreams under ancient willow

it hurts in places
beyond forever
not known to me until now

sunflowers bowing
my head full of dark debris
ancient dusty souls

you came at midnight
at dawn it was lost
fireplace warmth and the moonlight

an aging soul cries
teary puffy eyes
memories that lingers on

asleep with the moon
dusty dark storm clouds
breathe with sunflowers at noon

fragmented moonlight
tea ceremony
tears dancing down my rosy cheeks

pain needs our presence
healing is painful
pain is a long lonely road

unfolding healing
writing my story
my face lit by candlelight

often we feel lost
solace speaks softly
when the world gets too noisy

*I hold on to hope
it is all I have
even though my heart aches now*

www.ingramcontent.com/pod-product-compliance
Lightning Source LLC
Chambersburg PA
CBHW042043290426
44109CB00001B/20